Job + Real Estate = Wealth

Job + Real Estate = Wealth®

A Guide to Part-Time
Residential Property Investing

FRANCIS FERNANDO

RentMatch New Hampshire, LLC
259 Hanover Street
Manchester, NH 03104
www.francisfernando.com

Printed in the United States of America
First Printing, 2013

ISBN-13: 978-0615957456
ISBN-10: 0615957455

DEDICATION

This book is dedicated to my entire family.
You, I truly do care for and love.

CONTENTS

A Note from the Author   1

Acknowledgments   3

Introduction   5

Part I:
The Best Investor Mind-Set   **13**

Chapter 1: Confirming Your Choice: Why
Real Estate?   15

Chapter 2: Blending Personality Types for
Investment Success   19

Chapter 3: Making Smart Decisions With the
Business Process Wheel   27

Chapter 4: Scaling Your Plan and Your Business to
Maximize Returns and Future Growth   39

Chapter 5: Understanding the Roles of the
Real Estate Agent, Insurance Agent, Banker,
and Property Manager   47

Part II:
The Financial Benefits of Residential Real
Estate Investing   **55**

Chapter 6: Understanding Cash Flow, Leverage,
and Capital Appreciation   57

Chapter 7: Reaping the Tax Rewards of Real
Estate Investing   61

Part III:
Getting Started   **67**

    Chapter 8: Using Numbers-Based Proformas to
    Identify Strong Investment Properties   69

    Chapter 9: Lining Up a Property Manager   85

    Chapter 10: Working with Insurance Agents to
    Get the Best Rates Possible   91

    Chapter 11: Presenting the Property to the Bank
    to Secure a Loan   95

    Chapter 12: Working with your Real Estate Agent
    to Make an Offer   99

Conclusion   103
Glossary   105

LIST OF FIGURES

Figure 1: Potential Returns from Rental
Real Estate vs. Stock/CD   15

Figure 2: The Business Process Wheel   28

Figure 3: Scalability   39

Figure 4: Example of Cash Flow   58

Figure 5: Leverage   59

Figure 6: Overview of Investment   63

Figure 7: The Conventional Buying Process   70

Figure 8: Property Proforma: Basic Information 73

Figure 9: Building Income   74

Figure 10: Total Operating Expenses   78

Figure 11: Performance Metrics   81

Figure 12: Letter to a property manager   86

Figure 13: Insurance Company Letter   92

Figure 14: Letter to a Banker   96

Figure 15: Letter to Real Estate Agent   100

A NOTE FROM THE AUTHOR

Welcome! My name is Francis Fernando and I am the creator of a very successful approach called *Job + Real Estate = Wealth*. In the pages that follow, I will show you a highly effective way to invest in residential real estate (e.g., multiunit apartment buildings) to supplement your existing income using finely tuned methods that will also allow you to keep your primary job.

Everywhere we turn, we are bombarded by messages about get-rich-quick investment schemes. "Buy real estate with no money down!" and "Flip that house and make a quick $100,000.00!" and (my all-time favorite) "Quit your job, invest in real estate, and you've just created your path to wealth."

Please be aware that in reality, most of these messages are a recipe for disaster. In particular, the one thing I will not ask you to do is quit your job. Your key to a secure financial future is to maintain your current career (or one like it) because it will serve as a stabilizing force while you systematically build your real estate investment portfolio.

The approach you will learn here is the culmination of my years of experience. It takes hard work, it takes dedication, it takes a process that is loaded with education and awareness—and, yes, it takes even a little luck. I'm glad you're here. Now let's begin!

ACKNOWLEDGMENTS

The path to writing *Job + Real Estate = Wealth* took many valuable turns. Through these, what I would call hairpin-turns, the content was always kept together by my amazing editor Renee Nicholls. Special thanks to Janna Hartley from Monguin Creative for the design, layout, images and proofreading of this book.

To Steve Gamlin, Mike Dolpies and Tim Benoit for setting me sail on the journey of authoring this book; to Stephen Boyd of Wadleigh Starr & Peters for the trademark, copyright and legal advice.

To my wife, Kishanie, who is my partner in marriage, business and in life; Tristan & Luke, my two wonderful boys for making me laugh everyday.

Thank you Barbara Corcoran, Paul Boynton, Christopher Thompson and Tony Roxo for the valuable advice. I have grown a great deal by observing each of you.

And of course, I am indebted to my father and mother, Adolphus & Vesta Fernando for instilling the values of education, hard work and humbleness in to my life.

INTRODUCTION

In this book, I'm going to show you how to keep your primary job, invest in residential real estate, and achieve financial freedom. I've written this book based on my firsthand experience both as a property investor and as the owner of a successful property management company.

I began to invest in real estate twelve years ago while maintaining my corporate job as a Senior Engineer for Verizon Communications. Today, in addition to managing my own residential real estate investments, I lead my company, Total Solutions Property Management in Manchester, New Hampshire, and manage nearly 500 residential units for clients across the nation and around the world.

Often times, I get a lot of calls from potential clients who tell me they just graduated from real estate investment programs like Robert Kiyosaki's and Dave Lindahl's and would like to buy some property. My question to them is always the same: "Why haven't you?"

They invariably respond, "Well, I don't have the time, I don't have the resources, and quite honestly, I don't know how."

Despite what you might expect, it is actually no big

surprise that these folks just graduated from prominent real estate programs like Robert Kiyosaki or Dave Lindahl but still don't feel prepared to buy property. Now, don't get me wrong. These schools have great programs. Some of their concepts particularly intrigue me, such as their advice to partner or syndicate and purchase real estate with others. But such broad ideas can be hard to implement, particularly if you're just starting out. The key for beginners is to learn how to invest in your market at a grassroots level. And that is exactly what my approach is all about.

Believe me: It IS possible to keep your primary job and supplement your primary income by investing in real estate. In the pages that follow, I'll show you how.

This book will give you a comprehensive skill-set—as well as the tools, confidence, and intuition to create a supplemental stream of income by investing in residential real estate. My approach is truly like no other!

I have broken the book up into three components. In Part I, I'll help you to prepare your mind-set before you invest. The proper mind-set is critical, because, if you take your first step with the wrong attitude, it can result in a costly mistake that might prevent you from taking any further steps.

At the start of this section, we'll review different personality types and examine the strengths that you'll need for successful business transactions. I will also discuss the process of developing a game plan on how to identify, secure, measure, and support your investment. Specifically, you'll learn how to use the Business Process Wheel to make effective decisions as you move forward. We'll also look at the importance of scaling your plan so that you can grow your investments at an attainable level. Finally, we'll examine the functions of the people who will play key roles in your investment plan: your real estate agent, insurance agent, banker, and (potentially) property manager.

In Part II, we will discuss the financial benefits of residential real estate investing. You will gain an understanding of the powers of cash flow, leverage, capital appreciation, and tax benefits associated with real estate. This will give you the knowledge you'll need to view potential investments from a financial versus emotional perspective.

In Part III, we are going to roll up our sleeves and really get into the tools of real estate investing. Specifically, I will

- Teach you to use a very efficient tool called a *proforma* to determine if a property is a good investment or not;

- Show you how to select and manage your property manager;

- Show you how to attain the best quote from your insurance agent;

- Show you how to present your property to a bank to get the best interest rate;

- Show you how to work with a real estate agent to make an offer that is supported by actual numbers.

A Few Disclaimers

I've said it before but I'll say it again. As you read through this book, please keep in mind that this approach to residential property investment is not a "get-rich-in-one-minute" scheme. There is no product that gets you rich in one minute! Real estate requires the mind-set of long-term investing. Moreover, in real estate, you really have to understand what you are doing since either you will be self-managing the assets or you will be managing the property manager. But that's why I'm here. If you take the time to carefully implement what you'll learn in this book, you will achieve success!

Throughout the book, you will find real-life examples to help you see what the process looks like in action. All of these examples are based on people I've worked with or situations I've encountered personally. However, to ensure the privacy of the individuals involves, all names and places have been altered.

One more disclaimer. While I will touch on a variety of subjects in this program, I am not an economist, I am not an accountant, I am not an attorney, and I am not a statistician. I am an engineer who worked the corporate lifestyle for eleven years before deciding to invest in real estate. I am an engineer by background with a love for business and process. So for specific legal and financial issues, you will also want to consult with experts in those fields.

The Story Behind Job + Real Estate = Wealth

Before I start to teach you the skills you'll need to move forward, let me explain how I formed the basis for my approach: *Job + Real Estate = Wealth*. In my case, the *Job*, which used to be my engineering career, is currently my property management business, where I work hard each day to handle the day-to-day interests of the property owners whom I represent. The *Real Estate* consists of the properties that I have invested in personally and that I am responsible for owning—just as you will be responsible for yours. And the *Wealth* is the supplemental income that these purchases are generating, which of course is also the ultimate goal for any investments that you will make. Here's a quick look at how it all started.

In 2003, I was working full-time as an engineer with Verizon. Without any idea of whether or not my goals were even achievable, I set out with the grand plan that I was going to build a portfolio of 100 residential units. That year, I bought a five-family apartment building. I also set the goal of buying an additional building every subsequent year.

As part of this plan, in 2004, I bought a six-family apartment building. Now I was up to eleven residential units. At that point, I was still able to keep up with my corporate job, with enough extra time to take care of building maintenance and show vacant apartments. I was traveling for my day job and making supplemental money on the rental income. Life was good! Then when 2005 came around, I decided to step things up a bit and purchase a larger, eight-unit apartment building.

That's when things started to get hard for me. This building had some stability issues in terms of retaining tenants, and that issue needed attention. There were several vacancies, the existing tenants rarely paid their rent on time, and the rents were far below the market value since the previous owner hadn't raised them for years. Without a scalability plan—a way to keep my job *and* keep my investments running smoothly—I found myself putting a great deal of my Verizon paycheck into each of these buildings, and I did not know how to get the money back so I could keep reinvesting it in real estate.

Before I knew it, I was financially and logistically stuck. I found myself daily in situations where I was working and traveling and constantly fielding calls from residents complaining about maintenance and leasing issues. "I have no hot water." "I can't pay my rent because my mom died." Plus I was not available to show the vacant apartments to prospective tenants.

Between 2005 and 2006, my investment "plan" took a sharp nosedive as the vacancy rates went up and my collected income went down. As noted, I was unable to keep up with apartment showings when there were vacant apartments, and worst of all, I was using the income from my job to support the buildings.

Today, I see many investors who find themselves in a similar situation. Sadly, many don't realize their options, so they throw-in- the-towel and sell their investment properties. As you will see, however, with the right planning it is indeed possible to have a job *and* keep investment properties. Back in 2006, I just needed to figure out how.

At the time, I was not able to find a management company that met the criteria I felt was essential. (We'll discuss this criteria later in the book.) Consequently, I made the decision to leave my corporate job so I could step up to the plate and manage my buildings. However, quitting your job is actually a step that I advise you *not* to take. As I soon discovered, even though I suddenly had all the time in the world to take care of my properties, the supplemental rent money was not enough to serve as the main source of income for me and my family.

It is also difficult to get future loans if you do not have a primary source of income. By polling several loan officers and underwriting committee members, I learned that the number one thing that bank officers look at to determine if they are comfortable in granting a loan is the presence of a reliable stream of income from a job. A job offers dignity, ability, and stability, which makes you "bankable."

These two issues are the main reasons I advocate the job aspect of *Job + Real Estate.* Unless you are independently wealthy, as a part-time real estate investor you really do need to have a primary job.

As I soon discovered, the key is to find the balance to make both elements (*Job + Real Estate*) work. In my case, I decided to keep my investment properties and restore the *Job* element by creating a new career for myself, one that would fulfill the needs of struggling part-time investors just like me. That's how my company, Total Solutions Property Management was born.

When I founded this firm to manage the properties of my clients (my new *Job*) as well as my own (my *Real Estate*), I was able to fine-tune my approach to residential real estate investing (*Wealth*).

Remember, *Job + Real Estate = Wealth.*

Let's dive in to the heart of the book now, and I'll show you how it's done.

PART I

The Best Investor Mind-Set

As you start to explore the skills and tools for residential property investment, it's important to make sure that you're starting off on the right foot. We all have friends and family who have jumped into some type of business without having thought things through. Sometimes these folks do really well and they are a source of inspiration. Sometimes these folks do really poorly and deter us from trying the same thing. In most cases, whether they succeed or fail, their final outcome is based on a rocky foundation called "luck."

Developing the correct mind-set will help you avoid such risks. It will allow you to start off with your best foot forward and ensure that you can handle the challenges involved with managing the synergies of holding a primary job while investing in real estate as a supplemental source of income.

CHAPTER 1
Confirming Your Choice: Why Real Estate?

Sometimes people ask me why they should invest in real estate versus stocks or CDs. Figure 1 contains the numbers I usually show them.

Cash Available = $72,000.00

Choice = Stocks/CD or Rental Real Estate

Fair Assumption = 10% return on value for both the Stock/CD or Real Estate

Return: Rental Real Estate

$360,000.00 x 10% = $36,000.00 return
+ $72,000.00 original investment
Year 1 Cash Out = $108,000.00

Return: Stock/CD

$72,000.00 x 10% = $7,200.00 return
+ $72,000.00 original investment
Year 1 Cash Out = $79,200.00

Figure 1: Potential Returns from Rental Real Estate vs. Stock/CD

For the purposes of this example, let's say you have $72,000.00 to invest. Further, let's make the reasonable assumption that both products (real estate vs. a stock or CD) are going to yield a 10 percent return on value in year one. So, if you purchase a stock with your $72,000.00 you receive a $7,200.00 return on your investment in year one.

$72,000.00 x .10 = $7,200.00 *return on your investment*

If you cash out after one year, you get your original sum of money plus your 10 percent return. Your net year one cash out is $79,200.00.

$72,000.00 + $7,200.00 = $79,200.00 *year one cash out*

Now consider if you take that $72,000.00 to purchase real estate instead. Here, you will see the power of leverage. Your $72,000.00 will qualify you to use it as a 20 percent down payment on a $360,000.00 piece of real estate.

.20 x $360,000.00 *property* = $72,000.00 *down payment*

The beauty of this investment is that the capital appreciation—the rise in the asset's value based on a rise in market price—is not based upon your down payment of $72,000.00; it's based on **the entire value of the building**.

Let's say your property appreciates at 10 percent of the original price, which is $360,000.00.

$360,000.00 x .10 = $36,000.00 *year one return*

This means that at the end of the first year, the property is worth $396,000.00.

$360,000.00 + $36,000.00 = $396,000.00 *new property worth*

If you add your original $72,000.00 investment to the $36,000.00 year one return, your year one cash out is $108,000.00.

$72,000.00 + $36,000.00 = $108,000.00 *year one cash out*

Compare that to your $79,200.00 cash out playing the stock market.

Additionally, if your property is a rental building and it is managed correctly, your leveraged position of $360,000.00 (i.e., the $288,000.00 mortgage) is being paid down by your tenants. You're not using your own money to pay off your leveraged position—and that's the true beauty of residential real estate investing.

There is another big advantage to keep an eye on as you consider investments in real estate: demographic changes. For many people the long-term goal of owning a house is shifting, and globally, we are fast becoming a society of renters. It's a tangible reason to get into real estate, and this shift is going to become even more pronounced over the next ten to twenty years.

More detailed information about the financial benefits of residential real estate investing appears in Part II. For now, let's take a quick look at how cultivating certain business personality traits can help you make the best investment choices.

CHAPTER 2
Blending Personality Types for Investment Success

In my travels and business dealings, I've come across what I call five different business personality types. People with the first four personality types, which range from *Stick to My Comfort Zone* to *Leap Before I Look*, may run into trouble as residential property investors (if they get that far at all). If you recognize any of these characteristics in yourself, consider taking steps to fine-tune your business approach as needed to hurdle past attitudes that may hold you back and to ensure that you can meet your goals. As you will see, the ideal residential property investor blends the best qualities of these four personality types into a new, fifth type, which you can adopt to help you succeed.

Type 1: Stick to My Comfort Zone

The first personality type I've encountered is the person who does nothing new. These are folks who are just comfortable with what they're doing and are content with the status quo.

I am going to use a former coworker from Verizon as an example. Lisa and I used to sit in a cubicle right next to each other. Lisa would come in to work every single day at exactly the same time. She would eat the same lunch every day, and she would even drink from the same coffee mug. Socially, she had no real interest in broadening her horizons or trying anything new. People like that are happy with the status quo.

Since you have taken the steps to research investing by picking up this book, it's highly unlikely that you fall into this first personality type. However, if you do identify yourself as Stick to My Comfort Zone, that's ok too. You may just need to get some extra support to move you out of your comfort zone long enough to make the initial purchase.

In fact, after that initial purchase, people like Lisa often do well with real estate specifically because it's a long-term investment approach. People with the qualities of Type 1 have the patience to stick through the highs and lows of real estate investing without throwing in the towel. That patience is the key ingredient you'll wish to add to the blended personality type (Type 5).

Type 2: Paralysis by Analysis

The second personality type is distinguished by what is known as "paralysis by analysis." People like this analyze everything to a paralyzing extent. They surround themselves with charts and spreadsheets, but they can never seem to put a plan into action.

I have a friend named Mike who works as an engineer. We were colleagues for many years, and Mike always had a lot of big ideas about opening up his own business. Every day he would show me his charts and spreadsheets, and exclaim over the income he could potentially make.

One of his ideas was to establish a brokerage company for mortgages and create funds for people who purchase unstable real estate that a bank would not finance. His plan involved taking a fee for introducing a moneylender to the borrower, and he also intended to earn a percentage of the income. It was a great idea and the numbers looked right, but Mike spent all of his time on his charts and spreadsheets and failed to take any action.

People like Mike need to take steps to move beyond analysis and into firm action if they wish to success at residential property investment. Working with a business coach or counselor may help.

The good news is that a reasonable level of analysis is a very important skill for property investors to develop. As you will see, property investors need to be able to analyze potential properties with the same mind-set of an insurance agent, and, during the purchase process in particular, there are plenty of numbers to crunch and details to check to ensure that the deal will pay off. That balanced level of analysis is the character trait you'll want to develop for the blended personality, Type 5.

Type 3: All Talk, No Action

The third personality type describes people who talk about plans but don't even make it to the analysis stage. People like this can really get under your skin. My wife and I have an acquaintance named Kathy who falls into this third category. Our kids play sports together, so I see her all the time at games. Kathy has a lot of grandiose plans, but she's never analyzed her goals at all. She dreams of starting a public speaking career and inspiring people to get into business, but whenever I ask her if she has done any analysis or come up with a marketing plan, she doesn't even know what I'm asking.

There are a lot of people like this—folks who will have a different idea every time you see them. As with the Type 2 personality, if you find yourself to be in this category you may want to work with a life coach or other advisor before you start the process of investing in residential real estate. Such support can help you actually get the show on the road—and stay there.

As with the first two types, there are actually some positive qualities to take away here. People who love to talk about their ideas are usually very personable. As a property investor, you will need to form a solid relationship with your banker, real estate agent, and other professionals, not to mention your tenants. The elements of friendliness, creativity, and approachability are the qualities you'll want to take with you here.

Type 4: Leap Before I Look

Additionally, there are people who chase their dreams without any analysis or real plan. But to their credit, they do take action! These people are interesting because they can influence you in two very different ways. Their success can serve as a tremendous inspiration, or their failures may seem like a crippling warning against trying.

An old college buddy, Stephen, is very much like this. After we left college, Stephen went through a series of jobs with varied degrees of success. Currently, Stephen has a business salvaging old cars and fixing them up. He documents the restoration process on YouTube and sells the restored vehicles for substantially less than the market value. Customers love it because they have full disclosure on the car's condition before the restoration process, and they are buying the car at a great value.

But here's the thing. Prior to this, Stephen did not really know much about restoring cars. He simply jumped into it. In this case, he was able to land on his feet, but to succeed in real estate investment, it's really important to understand precisely what you're getting into.

If you have this personality type, you will need to learn to keep your impulses in check as you consider buying properties. Otherwise, you may end up spending a lot of money only to discover later on that you are stuck with a clunker in need of expensive repairs.

Still, unlike the first three personality types, you'll have no problem getting the ball rolling and diving in. Sometimes good deals need immediate action. That sense of energy and excitement is what you'll want to take into the blended personality.

Type 5: Blended Personality

Someone with the "blended" personality has just the right amount of staying power, confidence, analysis, intuition, people skills, and energy—the precise qualities that you will need to develop if you are going to keep your day job and start investing in real estate.

This fifth personality type helped me find the path to success when I formed Total Solutions Property Management several years ago. Let's take a look at how each attribute helped me.

- *Staying power.* When I first started to invest in real estate, I wanted to make sure I always had a "sure thing" to fall back on. At the time, I had almost paid off the condo I was living in. I decided that as I moved forward and bought more properties, I would make sure I always kept my condo. That way, if my investments didn't work out for some reason, I would always have a paid-off home to move back to. Fast forward to the present, and I still own that "safety net"—which I now rent to tenants—today.

- *Confidence.* As an engineer, I knew I had the right skills to bring to real estate investment. In particular, I recognized that my sharp focus on process and systems would translate very well. Over time, I was able to use these skills to hone the approach I will share in this book.

- *Analysis.* When I made the decision to trade my engineering job for self-employment based on the rental real estate market, my children were young. It felt like a huge risk for me to step outside of the corporate world, where I was making significant income, and place my focus on real estate. I was entering unknown territory, just as you may be doing when you consider your first investment. How did I do it? I did it with just the right amount of analysis. I didn't allow myself to excessively fixate on my spreadsheets, but I did make sure that I had a solid business plan.

- *Intuition.* I also had the right amount of gut feeling. I felt positive about my idea and discussed it with my wife, who confirmed that I seemed to be on track. While I would never advise you to rely on intuition exclusively, over time you will find that as a supplemental tool, it can help you consider new investments and deal with tenants and members of your core support team.

- And speaking of those tenants and team members, that's where strong *People Skills* come into play. As I continue to invest in properties, I need to work with bankers, real estate agents, and so forth. My people skills allow me to do this with ease.

- *Energy.* In this case, energy refers both to physical and mental energy. First, it's essential to have the physical resources to add part-time investing to a full-time job. To keep myself healthy, I make sure I eat well, and I schedule in time to work out. Second, as I've noted, it's critical to have the mental energy to move beyond the status quo. As I continue to look for good investment deals, I often find that it's necessary to make decisions and take action on tight deadlines.

All of these final personality traits will be essential to moving forward with your plan. Now let's take a look at a very useful tool that will help you make great decisions as a residential real estate investor.

CHAPTER 3
Making Smart Decisions With the Business Process Wheel

Now that you've discovered the benefits of developing a blended personality type, the next step is to learn a tool that will help you create concrete, effective plans for your future investments.

As you may know, engineers are very process-driven. During my eleven-year career at Verizon, the concept of "process" was my mantra. Every time I was faced with a problem, I ran that situation through a tool that I called my *business process wheel* (Figure 2).

This concept has been a true inspiration to me. Not only did it help me make important engineering decisions back then, but I use this tool today to help with the essential planning that is required to

- Keep my existing residential real estate investments running smoothly, and

- Help me make decisions about future investments.

As the figure shows, the business process wheel takes you through the four major steps of the decision-making process.

1. Identify

2. Execute

3. Measure

4. Support

Process Wheel

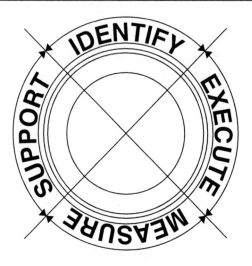

Figure 2: The Business Process Wheel

As the following examples show, you can use the business process wheel to make smart decisions whether you are just getting started, are in the midst of buying a property, or are evaluating whether your existing investment is working as well as it should. In fact, since at times you may need to make several decisions pretty much simultaneously, you may find yourself using several different process wheels at the same time—one for each decision. Let's talk briefly about each of the elements on the wheel.

Step 1: Identify

For this first example, let's say that you are about to step into the world of investing. To begin, you will need to take steps to **identify** your specific investment strategy. You can't invest in every type of real estate that's out there, so you will have to narrow down your focus. Specifically, you will need to decide if you wish to invest in commercial real estate (e.g., restaurants, malls, and convenient stores) or residential real estate (e.g., homes and apartment buildings). Within residential real estate, which is what this book focuses on, there are also many subgroups (e.g., condominiums, single-family homes, and apartment buildings).

Since you've picked up this book, you are probably interested in residential real estate, so let's say that you identify your target as a four-unit apartment building. Next, you need to identify if you want to purchase a property that is *stable* or *unstable.*

Stable properties have a consistent cash-flow basis month after month. These properties are able to output a consistent, steady stream of cash due to the fact that the tenant base is stable and there is very little or no deferred maintenance on the property. These are buildings that will not likely demand much else from you in terms of additional time, resources, or money beyond the purchase price; they are pretty much turn-key properties and are usually priced accordingly.

On the other hand, unstable properties have a pattern

of consistent tenant move-outs and move-ins, as well as unpredictable cash flow output due to the patterns in which tenants have been allowed by previous building owners to pay (or not pay!) rents. Furthermore, the properties are typically riddled with maintenance issues that are in need of immediate attention. In some cases, these properties can be a bargain if you have the time, resources, and money needed to step in and make them stable again. They can also become a huge headache if you do not.

You might use a different process wheel to help you plan out your long-term goal for the investment. (As noted, you can create different process wheels for each step you need to take, each decision you need to make, or each problem you want to solve.) In this case, the first step would be to *identify* which approach you want to pursue.

1. *Short-term flipping.* You've probably seen television programs in which investors purchase a house that needs work, fix it up, and then resell it for a profit.

2. *Repositioning.* Some investors choose to purchase rental units that are floundering. Maybe the building is full of vacancies or tenants who don't pay the rent in a timely manner. These properties also typically have deferred maintenance issues such as functionally obsolete amenities (e.g., large intrusive parlor heaters). The investor corrects these issues and could, like flipping, sell the improved property within a relatively short timeframe to make a quick profit. Alternately, the investor could keep the property to benefit from the newly created cash flow stream.

3. *Syndication.* This is a type of investment plan that is

often mentioned at real estate investment courses. With syndication, investors who would not have the money or experience to buy a large number of units or an apartment complex independently team with other investors to make the purchase and share any income generated from the building.

4. *Traditional investing.* With this approach, investors buy residential real estate and then hold it for the long term, with the specific aim of benefitting from the monthly cash flow and the increased value of the property over time.

We will focus on the fourth approach in this book, with some touches of the second approach.

As I mentioned, you can also use the process wheel to help you make smart decisions while you are in the midst of buying a property or while you are dealing with issues about an existing investment. For instance, once you've found a property to buy, as you plan financing you might use a wheel to identify what type of mortgage you want to pursue and/or which banks you might wish to approach.

Similarly, after you have purchased the property, you might use a wheel to identify what upgrades you'd like to implement, and so forth. The basic idea is that any time you find yourself faced with a problem or in need of a decision, you can use a wheel to first identify exactly what needs to occur and then—through *execute, measure, and support*—follow through effectively.

Step 2: Execute

Once you've identified what needs to occur, the next step is to **execute** your plan. This will vary based on the approach you've identified as the one you wish to take. For instance, in the execution stage, someone who has identified that she wants to buy and reposition a property will focus on finding a property in need of improved management. In contrast, someone who has identified that he'd like to take the traditional approach will focus on finding a property that will generate income and increase in value over time.

Similarly, someone who has identified upgrades she wishes to make to an existing investment building will start interviewing contractors and getting estimates. Someone who is in the midst of stabilizing a tenant base may take steps to reeducate tenants on the payment policies. The point is to *act on* whatever issue you've identified in the first part of the wheel.

Unfortunately, many people fail in the execution phase and never move beyond identifying their plan. In my experience, this is because they always seem to find excuses to keep them from actually executing their plan. Typical excuses I hear at this stage are, "I don't have enough time," or "I'm traveling too much right now," or "I have a lot of stress at work." In the execute phase, it is essential that you take the time to work on the steps that will make your plan a success.

Step 3: Measure

The next step in the wheel is to **measure** the outcome of the execution. This allows you to assess whether you're still on track or if you need to make some adjustments moving forward.

For instance, let's say that ten years ago you created a process wheel in which you identified that you wanted to have six lucrative properties by the time you turned forty-five. Over the years, you have taken steps to execute this. Now, on your forty-fifth birthday, you will measure if you have achieved this or not.

As another example, let's say that, in the execution phase, you took steps to reeducate your tenants about the payment process (after you identified that the rent was often late). You created a handout highlighting when the rent is due, where it should be sent, and what consequences will be taken if it's late. A few months later, you would measure the effectiveness of the handout by checking to see if more tenants have paid the rent on time.

Depending on the issue that has been identified and the approach that has been executed, measures can be financial (e.g., "$20,000.00 annually in cash flow") or personal ("financial freedom to send my kids to the college of their choice") or simply practical ("getting the lawn mowed at the property every week"). As an investor, you'll have both short-term and long-term measures. For example, depending on the goal you've tried to execute, you may decide to assess your success by looking at quarterly cash flow, long-term impacts to your tax bracket, and so forth. The main thing is to evaluate the success or failure of the execution so you can learn from any mistakes and adjust your strategy accordingly as you move forward.

Step 4: Support

The final step is **support**, which boils down to a simple question.

Do I have a system in place to clear any obstacles that arose as part of my execution process and/or were revealed when I measured the results?

For this example, let's start with the big picture, in which the goal is for you to be able to keep your day job for your primary source of income and then invest in residential real estate as a source of supplemental income. To achieve that, you will need to have an effective support system in place to help you overcome any obstacles that might otherwise prevent you from keeping your job and handling your investments. Whether the potential obstacles involve your job, stress, or travel, it is key to know how you can work through those issues and support your investment strategy.

Here's another example. Let's say you own a property and you're responsible for mowing the lawn. However, you find that with your busy work and family life, you are constantly struggling to fit this task in. For support, you decide to adapt a method that I've found works well for task management, the "batch work" principle proposed by author Tim Ferriss. This involves dividing your time so that you focus on a single task for a certain period versus constantly switching tasks.

Following Ferriss's approach, you decide to simply designate a certain time for "property yard maintenance" and then honor it week after week. You choose Saturday mornings at 9 a.m., when you know that your kids will still be in their pajamas watching cartoons, which means you won't miss out on quality family time. With this method, you will always know when you're going to mow the lawn, and you won't schedule anything else for that time. With this support system in place, you start to manage the task, versus letting the task manage (and overwhelm!) you.

You can also apply Ferriss's approach to your job to ensure that you work efficiently and have time to look after your investment. You may also need to set up boundaries regarding leaving time and travel time so that you are free to care for the property. Alternately, you may want to think about the effectiveness of hiring a property manager, which we will discuss in more detail later in the book. Again, the primary goal is to ensure that you have the necessary supports in place to ensure that you are always driving your behavior and your approach to your investment, instead of letting it drive you.

Let's take a quick look at an example that shows how this tool worked to help a friend of mine become a very successful residential real estate investor.

The Process Wheel in Action

Step 1: Identify

Joe's initial objective was to match his income as a regional sales manager with the supplemental income he could gain by building a real estate portfolio. Joe had a clear sense of direction, and he identified his initial target property as an apartment building with six or more units that was considered unstable.

Step 2: Execute

Next, Joe developed an execution strategy to meet this goal. He knew that properties with five or more units required a commercial loan, so he began by forming a core support team that included a banker whose specialty was the commercial financing of properties that needed stabilizing. He also chose a real estate agent who was well versed in searching out bank-owned and/or unstable investment properties; an insurance agent who understood and appreciated the course and path towards stabilizing an investment property; and, of course, a property manager who knew how to implement a repositioning project. He ran the numbers through an analysis tool called a proforma (see Chapter 8), obtained a low-rate mortgage from the bank, and purchased a six-unit apartment building that met his criteria. Then, over time, he successfully stabilized it.

Step 3: Measure

After Joe identified and executed his plan, he measured the success he had meeting his goals to stabilize the property and to generate a certain amount of income from his real estate business. He measured the net cash flow that each rental unit generated for him, and he was delighted to discover that the measure exceeded his original intention and his strategy.

Step 4: Support

How did Joe support this strategy? He surrounded himself with the right team, including the right bank, real estate agent, insurance agent, and property management company. And he didn't merely surround himself with his team, he *led* his team. Today, Joe owns a portfolio of 120 residential units, and Joe's supplemental income is $282,000.00. That is his net profit, by the way! He was able to more than double his income (which was his original goal), without needing to deal with the operational aspects of his business because he has a property management company to oversee those details.

As this chapter has shown, whether you are trying to meet the long-term objective of attaining a specific financial measure, or you are struggling to meet the immediate goal of taking care of your property's lawn, the process wheel can serve as an essential tool to help you reach success. In the next chapter, we'll look at more steps you can take to help you succeed as a residential real estate investor.

CHAPTER 4
Scaling Your Plan and Your Business to Maximize Returns and Future Growth

Now that you've had a quick look at how to develop and execute a plan using the steps in the process wheel, the next concept you'll want to embrace is *scalability* (Figure 3).

Scalability

Business Scalability is the systematic (process-oriented) ability to replicate or duplicate the desiredeconomic outcome of an initiative over and over again

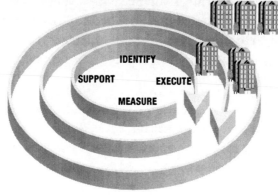

Figure 3: Scalability

As the figure explains, scalability is the process-oriented ability to replicate or duplicate the desired economic outcome of your plan over and over again.

At the most basic level, your scalability plan will involve ensuring that the supplemental income you receive from renting units is continuous. You want your investment to provide a steady return month after month and not be hindered by issues such as long-term vacancies, tenants who don't pay the rent, or your own lack of time to take care of issues. So the specifics of your scalability plan will involve the details of what you've identified as the desired outcome (e.g., monthly income, growth in property value, etc.) and precisely how you will execute, measure, and support your approach to achieve this.

In the broader picture, particularly as you become more experienced as an investor, you may wish to develop a scalability plan that allows you to purchase additional buildings in the future with the earnings you make from your property. Here, too, you would use the process wheel to identify the specific aim, the execution plan, the measurement tools, and the support you will need to gradually expand your residential real estate portfolio.

Scalability and process must go hand in hand. In other words, you can't have a scalable business plan unless you have a process to identify, execute, measure, and support it. And when you do have a good process, you should be able to scale your business an infinite number of times, which is how your investments will grow.

The previous chapter ended with Joe's success story. Now,

as a precaution, let's consider what may occur when you *don't* have a strong scalability plan. After that, we'll take a look at one of my favorite coffee shop franchises, which is a great example of a successful scalability plan in action.

A Cautionary Tale

About five years ago two friends, Kelly and Pat, *identified* their goal: to gain supplemental income by pooling their resources to purchase and self-manage a three-unit apartment building, and then eventually to use that income to purchase more buildings. Kelly was a physical therapist and Pat worked as a kindergarten teacher. In terms of *execution,* initially everything seemed to go smoothly, but then life got in the way.

The first problem arose when they no longer had time to do showings for prospective tenants. Kelly's workload frequently extended beyond fifty hours per week, and Pat was tied up with parent and staff meetings long after the school day would end. Soon their three-unit building had only one occupancy. Now they were bringing in only a third of their maximum income in rent. Financially, they started getting hurt. Each needed to put in part of her own paycheck just to cover the mortgage on the building. In terms of *measurement,* it was clear that their dream of building a property portfolio was quickly spiraling downhill.

Another problem concerned building maintenance. Every time they needed any work done on the units they would hire a contractor, but with no one there to manage the contractors, work didn't get done to their expectations.

Kelly and Pat's error was caused in part by the lack

of scalability of their plan. When they first considered residential real estate investing and made the purchase, they did not think about *support:* how they were going to manage the building and how much time and resources they had to allocate to property management.

Unfortunately, this is not an isolated example. My company often receives calls from new investors who forgot to plan how to support and scale their plan and thus have found themselves in over their heads. At that point, many are tempted to throw in the towel and sell their investment altogether.

Kelly and Pat ended up hiring a property management company to get their investment back on track. In terms of scalability, they now need to take an active role in leading their management team to ensure that their situation remains stable. Once this occurs, they may even be able to buy more properties in the future.

A Successful Scalability Plan in Action

In the previous chapter, we saw how Joe started with one six-unit apartment building and then, over time, was able to purchase other properties and increase his supplemental income substantially. Joe is a terrific example of a successful scalability plan in action. To gain an even bigger sense of how a scalability plan can eventually take an investor from a single entity to a growing empire, let's take a quick look at one of my favorite café and bake shops, Tim Hortons (or Timmies, as it's affectionately known in Canada).

To me, that morning cup of coffee sets the tone for the

day. In my case, it has to be just perfect, with the right color and temperature (large coffee, half teaspoon sugar, two milks – no cream). What initially impressed me about Tim Hortons was that no matter what Timmies I went to, whether I was visiting family in Buffalo, New York or Toronto, Canada, my cup of coffee and buying experience were extremely consistent. Consistency, in my opinion, was their brand.

In fact, I've been so impressed with their service that in my family circles it has become quite the tradition for me to leave whichever home I'm visiting early in the morning to enjoy a sole cup of coffee at Tim Hortons. Oftentimes, I will simply sit and observe the customer buying experience, and other times I will actually count the number of customers being served and then perform rudimentary mathematics to hypothesize what their daily sales would be. Initially, I think my family found the gesture of me having a solo cup of coffee a bit unsocial, but they did not realize just how impressed and intrigued I was by the Tim Hortons business model. When I looked into it a bit further, I realized it's the perfect example of a successful scalability plan.

This original business model was started in 1964 by Tim Horton, a National Hockey League All-Star defensemen. Over time, the business grew from its first location in Hamilton, Ontario, to 4,264 cafe and bake shops across Canada, the United States, and other international locations. In 1967, Tim Horton and Ron Joyce partnered and laid the foundation blocks for a process-orientated, rapidly-scalable business model that was implemented despite Tim Horton's tragic death in a car accident in 1974.

From the start of their partnership, the pair realized that

as strong as coffee and donut sales were, the scalable nature of it was limited to the output of their one physical restaurant. In other words, they would not be able to grow the business simply by increasing the operations of that one location. Instead, the expansion potential existed in their ability to buy more properties and enable franchisees to run the restaurants. In a snapshot here is their scalable solution:

1. As the franchisor, they receive 3 to 4.5 percent of gross sales from the franchisee of each location.

2. They own the real estate and, if not, control the master lease and lease or sublease the property to the franchisee. The typical lease rate is 8.5 to 10 percent of gross sales.

3. They also own the following centrally located profit centers: five distribution centers, two coffee roasting manufacturing facilities, and one fondant and filling manufacturing facility. Franchisees are required to purchase all product offerings from these centrally located facilities.

Basically, the owners of Tim Hortons identified their marketplace and determined the scalable and process-oriented business model that they were to follow – and, more importantly, persevered through it. Despite some roadblocks, they stayed the course of the foundations of how they identified themselves. They executed an aggressive growth plan and have measures-based market capitalization. Their support infrastructure, besides the vertically-integrated systems and processes, consists of their franchisees, who run the day-to-day operations of the cafe and bake shops.

JOB + REAL ESTATE = WEALTH

Your scalability plan does not need to be based on goals for cross-country expansion. But while future growth may be optional, *sustainable success* is essential. To avoid mistakes like Kelly and Pat's, before you purchase your first property you'll want to be sure to have a strong scalability plan in place. And as their story shows, that plan should include a strong, core-support team that's lead by *you*—a subject we'll discuss in the next chapter.

CHAPTER 5
Understanding the Roles of the Real Estate Agent, Insurance Agent, Banker, and Property Manager

After scalability, the next thing for you to think about is how to build the right team of experts to help you execute your plan and ensure that it's scalable. We've all been told that successful folks surround themselves with the smartest and most capable people. I agree with that concept—with one important addition. The fact is, you need to be able to *lead* the team that surrounds you. Otherwise, if you simply hand over the reins to a third party—whether that be your real estate agent, your property manager, or any other person—you may run into trouble later and discover that the outside individual either lacked the necessary know-how or did not really have your best interests at heart.

To lead your team successfully, you will need to understand exactly what they are meant to do. Specifically, you will want to learn about each of their industries, which is what this chapter will help you explore. When you know what the members of your team need from you, you will be able to offer the right support and guidance to help them do their jobs effectively.

FRANCIS FERNANDO

Let's take an insurance agent as an example. On the one hand, the insurance agent is someone you'll need on your team. Down the road you may have claims, and you will find that your property must meet certain requirements in order to qualify for insurance coverage at all.

However, you will not want to take a hands-off approach toward insurance (or any other matter that involves making the best choices for your investment). Instead, you will want to develop the skills and knowledge required for you to be able to think like an insurance agent yourself. For example, you will want to be able to inspect potential properties with a specific eye toward any issues that are likely to hike your insurance rates up (e.g., outdated electrical wiring). Once you are able to identify such issues up front, you can effectively negotiate the cost of repairs with the seller before you seal the deal, or you can make the educated decision to choose a different property to invest in instead.

In contrast, if you take a hands-off approach and wait for the insurance agent (or the insurance company's inspector) to identify such issues after you've made the purchase, then you will likely find yourself stuck with a property that has high insurance rates—or that can't be covered by long-term insurance until all costly repairs are done.

The bottom line is that you want to educate yourself about your investment as much as possible so you can lead your team and make informed decisions as you move forward.

Building Your Core Team

The members of your core success team as it applies to your real estate investments are

- Your **real estate agent,**
- Your **insurance agent**,
- Your **banker,** and potentially
- Your **property manager**.

We could identify others like attorneys or electricians, but for the success of your investment strategy, they are not part of your core team.

Let's take a quick look at each of these main roles. In Part III, we will discuss specific conversations you should have with each of these team members as part of the actual real estate purchasing process.

Real Estate Agents

As you work with real estate agents, your goal will be to drive what occurs, not to serve as a passive consumer of the real estate agents' services. To help you do this, you will want to understand the real estate agents' most "primal instinct"—what motivates them. And while most real estate agents certainly enjoy viewing properties and working with people, the bottom line that we're talking about now is how they get paid.

Real estate agents get paid for *facilitating* a transaction between a buyer (you) and the seller. They are responsible for establishing and/or negotiating a mutually agreeable price and terms for the property.

Consequently, the more information that you can provide to the real estate agent in terms of what type of property interests you, the better your transaction will be. You do not want to approach a real estate agent and say, "Oh, I'm thinking about buying a building I can rent out for some income" and then rely on the real estate agent to guess (or create) your exact needs. Rather, you want to come to the table and say, "I am looking for an X-unit apartment building that meets, or has the potential to meet, the following criteria: Capitalization Rate of X, Debt Service Coverage Ratio of Y and Cash Flow of Z." These measures and ratios of performance will be covered in Chapter 8. In terms of stability, "I don't mind if the property needs a few cosmetic upgrades, but I do not want anything that will require a Capital Expense budget greater than $C of upgrades. Please ensure that any properties we'll look at meet these criteria."

In Chapter 8, I will show you a tool to help you analyze properties just like this. With this approach, you will actively drive the real estate agents' behavior because you have designated exactly what you expect them to facilitate for you. More information about working with real estate agents appears in Chapter 12.

Insurance Agents

Likewise, with insurance agents, to get the best rates in insurance you need to be able to influence their behavior. In this case, the insurance agents' "primal instinct" is to make money in one of two ways.

1. By investing your premiums and making a gain, and

2. By taking in more premiums than they have to pay out in claims.

This means that you are going to get the lowest rates for the properties that are in the best condition (i.e., that are unlikely to be the cause of expensive insurance claims). Consequently, you will want to educate yourself on what issues the insurance companies consider a risk and make sure that such issues, if they exist in the property that interests you, are addressed by the seller before you finalize the sale or by yourself shortly thereafter. As an informed buyer, you will want to negotiate with the seller during the purchase process about the repair of any issues that will affect insurance rates; otherwise, you will likely get stuck with the cost of repairs and/or higher insurance premiums down the road. More details about what issues to look for appear in Chapter 10.

Bankers

Along the same lines, it's going to be essential for you to learn what drives your bank, specifically what drives the bank to give you a loan.

As it pertains to a mortgage, a bank makes money through fees such as loan acquisition fees, commitment fees, and so forth. More important, they obtain money either by servicing the mortgages themselves (keeping them in house) and making money on the yield spread, or by selling "quality mortgages" (those that are unlikely to turn into foreclosures) to the secondary mortgage market. Let's take a quick look at how this works.

Servicing the Loan In-House

Let's say the bank holds $700,000.00 in deposits, for which they are paying their customers' saving accounts an interest rate of 1 percent. You apply for a $700,000.00 loan, which they grant to you at an interest rate of 6 percent. This example is oversimplified, because of course the bank is required to maintain a certain depository reserve, but you can see how the bank is earning money from the difference between the interest they are paying to their savings customers (1 percent) and the interest they are acquiring from their loan customers (6 percent).

Selling the Loan to the Secondary Market

Let's take a look at the same scenario, except this time the bank is going to sell your loan in the secondary mortgage market to an entity such as Fannie Mae. In this case, the bank no longer has to wait twenty or so years to get the initial $700,000.00 back from you; Fannie Mae gives it to the bank immediately when Fannie Mae buys the loan. In addition, Fannie Mae gives the bank a percentage of the money up front as a type of commission, so the bank will actually be taking in more than $700,000.00. In most cases, the bank will also get income from servicing the loan (sending you the mortgage statements and so forth). *And,* now that the bank has the $700,000.00 back in its own pocket, it can lend that money to someone else and start the process all over again. Talk about scalability and leverage!

Whether the bank plans to service your loan in-house or sell it to a third party such as Fannie Mae, the bank's "primal instinct" is to approve only the loans that are highly unlikely to fail. Otherwise, they will either lose money (with an in-house loan) or damage their relationship with their third-party "customer" (e.g., Fannie Mae).

The bottom line here is that when you approach a

mortgage lender, it is key to show them up front that you are not a risk. You will want to highlight your stability and ability. Emphasize the fact that you have a job, so you will still be able to pay the mortgage if something unexpected happens, like a sudden high-vacancy rate. Also showcase other potential forms of income to cover emergencies, such as investments, lines of credit, banking relationships, and so forth. The point is to show that you will not be a risk for foreclosure. More information about working with lenders appears in Chapter 11.

Property Managers

Along the same lines, if you intend to hire a property manager, it will be essential for you to understand exactly what that role entails. In my experience, far too many investors skip this step. Instead, nearly every time I get calls from potential clients looking to hire my services, they ask me nothing more than how much my company will charge. That's the extent of our conversation because they don't know how to manage their team.

In terms of the "primal instinct," property managers make money based on three streams of income.

1. Management fees, which are tied to the gross collected revenue;
2. Leasing fees for advertising, showing, and leasing vacant units; and
3. Maintenance income that's charged for routine expenses (e.g., day-to-day repairs) and capital expenses (e.g., project-based work that adds longevity and value to the building).

Chapter 9 will help you learn what to look for as you select someone to work with. Again, the goal will be for you to come to the table as an informed client—one who understands how the management company makes money, which controls you may need to implement, and how you may wish to use incentives that are tied to the manager's performance.

As you can see, it's essential to take the time to learn your team's industries. Lack of knowledge and understanding can lead to very poor decisions in terms of hiring and working with your team. Each member will have a direct impact on how you do business and the ultimate success of your strategy. Understanding how they work and what they need will help you lead them most effectively.

Part II

The Financial Benefits of Residential Real Estate Investing

Now that we've examined some of the things you'll need to know as you begin to make decisions and to build your support team, let's take a look at the *Wealth* part of the equation. There is a longstanding perception that people have developed a lot of wealth from real estate, and this is usually how people first become interested in the idea. Donald Trump's empire and popular television shows like *Flip This House* showcase people who have built wealth from real estate and passed it on to their loved ones. This has led to a widespread, global affinity for the idea of investing in real estate as a way to build wealth.

Every time I introduce myself at a gathering, I make it a point to establish that I manage real estate. It always piques people's interest, and I often get reactions like, "Oh, wow, I've always wanted to get involved in real estate." Clearly, many people have an interest in this field.

With that in mind, it's essential to remember that the

process of residential real estate investing will involve your active participation. Real estate is a working asset. Unlike a stock, CD, or bond, which you purchase and someone else manages for you, real estate is an active entity. You will be very much involved in your real estate assets. Even if you choose to hire a property management company, you will still be heavily involved in what I call "managing the manager."

This section looks at the financial benefits of investing in residential real estate. While you may end up hiring an accountant to manage your books, it will be essential for you to understand the numbers and how they work so that you can make the best decisions and lead your core support team. This section provides an overview of cash flow, leverage, and appreciation, and of how the tax breaks work.

CHAPTER 6
Understanding Cash Flow, Leverage, and Capital Appreciation

Cash Flow

It is important to understand the practical, rather than emotional, reasons to get into real estate. Of course, the first reason is **cash flow**. Real estate offers cash flow better than any other investment product out there. Think of cash flow as the income from rent checks coming in after you subtract the internal expenditures from running the building, your property taxes, your insurance premium, and your mortgage payment. The money that is left is your profit, or cash flow (Figure 4.)

As Figure 4 shows, other factors that influence cash flow are *vacancy loss,* which involves the amount of income you lose when a unit stands vacant, and *economic loss*, which results from tenants who are occupying a space but are not paying their rent.

In this case, the cash flow is calculated as follows. First, take the adjusted gross income (the rent you were actually able to collect) and subtract the operating expenses (e.g., maintenance, electricity for common areas, etc.). This leaves you with your net operating income.

Cash Flow

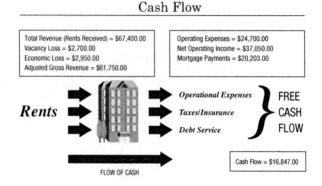

Total Revenue (Rents Received) = $67,400.00	Operating Expenses = $24,700.00
Vacancy Loss = $2,700.00	Net Operating Income = $37,050.00
Economic Loss = $2,950.00	Mortgage Payments = $20,203.00
Adjusted Gross Revenue = $61,750.00	

Figure 4: Example of Cash Flow

Adjusted gross revenue	$61,750.00
Operating expenses	-$24,700.00
Net operating income	$37,050.00

Since you have a mortgage payment, you now need to subtract that as well. What remains is your cash flow.

Net operating income	$37,050.00
Mortgage payments	-$20,203.00
Cash flow	$16,847.00

Chapter 6 shows how you can also use some of these figures to your advantage in the form of a tax deduction.

Leverage

The second reason why real estate is attractive centers on the concept of **leverage**. To illustrate this concept, let's take a quick look at leverage in engineering terms. Leverage is the mechanical advantage of moving an object using a lever. Try loosening the wheel bolts on your car with your bare hands and see how far you get. After that, try using the wheel wrench provided by the car manufacturer, and it's as easy as can be. The wrench acts as a lever and gives you a mechanical advantage.

In real estate, the primary source of leverage is bank financing (a mortgage). In Chapter 1, we looked at the different returns possible from a rental real estate investment vs. a stock or CD. This extended example (Figure 5) also highlights the value of leverage. You may not have the full purchase price on hand, but with the leverage—the ability to use bank financing—you are able to purchase a piece of expensive real estate that you wouldn't be able to purchase on your own.

Leverage

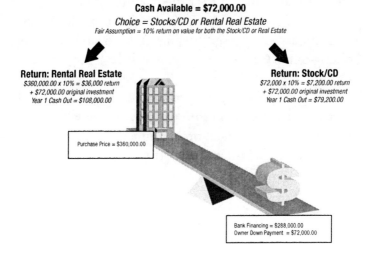

Figure 5: Leverage

Capital Appreciation

Capital appreciation is another way that you can benefit from residential real estate property investing. This term refers to the rise in the value of your property based on a rise in the marketplace.

During recent years, many of us have witnessed a decline in the value of some overinflated properties. This is a good reminder to buy properties with our heads (making strong financial decisions based on numbers) and not our hearts (making poor emotional decisions based on haste). Remember the personality types? Purchasing a property is definitely not the time to leap before you look.

With that in mind, historically most properties do increase in value over time—often significantly. Again, this is where some of the traits of the Comfort Zone personality type kick in. The approach used throughout this book focuses on buying a property and keeping it as an investment over the long-term. Consequently, you will be likely to benefit from capital appreciation as well as cash flow and leverage. Depending on your scalability plans, you may even find that the increased value of your property over time will help you gain more leverage in the form of future mortgages granted to you by banks for additional properties.

CHAPTER 7
Reaping the Tax Rewards of Real Estate Investing

The next advantage to going into real estate involves the tax benefits. Accountants often advise people to purchase a piece of real estate, but why is that? Why are tax write-offs important? Let's take a moment to consider the specific ways real estate investment affects your tax bracket.

To begin, it is important for you to really understand what a tax benefit is not. A tax write-off is not a refund. If I make a $300 charitable donation to the local animal shelter, it does not mean I'm going to get a $300 check from the government next April!

Instead, a tax write-off is a reduction in your taxable position based on money taken off the income you earn and report on your tax forms.

Let's take another look at that animal shelter donation. How does the write-off come into play? In this case, it means the taxable position on the income I earn and report has been reduced by $300—and that's only if the donation qualifies.

To reiterate, charitable donations—or in the case of

residential real estate investment, qualified business expenses and other factors such as depreciation—can be written off your income for an adjustment on your taxes, not for a check you'll get in the mail!

In the world of real estate, expenses and income related to your real estate ventures are recorded on a tax form that is called **Schedule E, Supplemental Income and Loss**. I encourage everyone interested in real estate to go online and print out a copy of the Schedule E tax form at *www.irs.gov/uac/Schedule-E-(Form-1040),-Supplemental-Income-and-Loss*.

Essentially, a Schedule E records every rent payment received and your total real estate income. It also gives you the ability to write off your business expenses.

The real beauty of the Schedule E centers around the two special write-offs it offers. One is called **depreciation**, which the IRS defines as "an annual allowance for the wear and tear, deterioration, or obsolescence of the property," and the second is your **mortgage interest**. Again, both of these write-offs are recorded on your Schedule E. Let's take a closer look at just how these write-offs work to benefit you.

For this example, let's consider our $360,000.00 investment again (Figure 6).

As you may recall, it has a total revenue of $67,400.00 in anticipated income. One unit was vacant for a period of time, giving us a vacancy loss of $2,700.00. For a few months, there was also a tenant actually occupying a space but not paying the rent. This economic loss, which amounted to $2,950.00, additionally took away from this building's potential revenue. This brought the **adjusted gross income (or adjusted gross**

revenue)—the money we were able to collect from this building—to $61,750.00.

Cash Flow

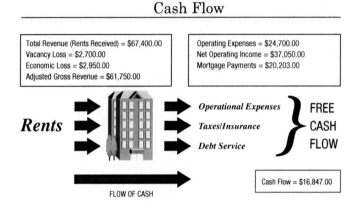

| Total Revenue (Rents Received) = $67,400.00 |
| Vacancy Loss = $2,700.00 |
| Economic Loss = $2,950.00 |
| Adjusted Gross Revenue = $61,750.00 |

| Operating Expenses = $24,700.00 |
| Net Operating Income = $37,050.00 |
| Mortgage Payments = $20,203.00 |

Rents

Operational Expenses

Taxes/Insurance

Debt Service

} FREE CASH FLOW

FLOW OF CASH

Cash Flow = $16,847.00

Figure 6: Overview of Investment

As we determined, going through the flow of cash, the next step was to factor in operating expenses. In this case, the operating expenses were $24,700.00. These expenses included maintenance, common area utilities, and landscaping.

The **net operating income** is the next thing to consider. This refers to the difference between the adjusted gross income ($61,750.00) and the total operating expenses ($24,700.00). In this case, the net operating income is $37,050.00. That is the money we cleared prior to paying the mortgage. This number will be recorded on Schedule E.

Now let's examine how depreciation and mortgage interest can reduce the amount of taxes you will have to pay on those earnings.

Depreciation

When we file our taxes, we can depreciate a physical building but not land. Let's say that on our building value of $360,000.00, the predetermined land value on the property is $60,000.00. So, the actual building value that can be depreciated is $300,000.00.

Building value to depreciate $300,000.00

The government allows property owners to depreciate a building over 27.5 years. So in this particular example, we have $300,000.00 divided by 27.5 years.

$$\$300,000.00 \div 27.5 = \$10,909.00$$

Thanks to the power of depreciation, this gives us an annual deduction of approximately $10,909.00 reduced from our taxable position.

NOTE: An important point to remember is that our original income reported on Schedule E is not the cash flow (which was calculated after we subtracted the mortgage payments), but a higher amount called the **net operating income** (which reflected what we took in before paying the mortgage). The potential tax liability that we would have paid without deductions for depreciation would have been $37,050.00, which was our net operating income, not our cash flow.

With the power of depreciation, our tax liability gets reduced by $10,909.00, bringing our taxable income to $26,141.00.

Net operating income	$37,050.00
Depreciation	-$10,909.00
Taxable income after deduction	$26,141.00

However, there is still one more tax write-off, and that's the mortgage interest deduction. Let's take a look at those figures next.

Mortgage Interest Deduction

In every mortgage payment that we make, there is a factor of principal that gets reduced, and there is a factor of interest that gets reduced. For our example, let's say it is broken out this way.

Total mortgage payments:	$20,203.00
$ applied toward principal:	$ 5,938.00
$ applied toward interest:	$14,265.00

Currently, the government allows property owners to reduce these accrued interest payments, which in this case was $14,265.00. Let's look at how this works.

First, let's go back to our taxable income of approximately $26,141.00 and subtract our mortgage interest ($14,265.00).

Taxable income	$26,141.00
Mortgage interest	-$14,265.00
New total for taxable income	$11,876.00

We are now paying taxes on an income of $11,876.00 even though the actual cash we got to take home (our cash flow) was $16,847.00. That's a $4,971.00 reduction on our tax burden!

PART III

Getting Started

Earlier in the book I mentioned that at my property management company, I often receive calls from potential clients who simply ask, "What will you charge to manage my property for me?" Unfortunately, many of the callers did not launch themselves into residential real estate ownership with a process or a plan. They may not have purchased the property with good interest and insurance rates—it probably depended on luck—and now they also don't know how to manage their investment or their core support team.

Unlike those callers, you are already an active, educated participant in your future investments. You have learned about planning, scalability, and the financial numbers and process that will be most important to you.

Now it's time to look at how you can put those plans into action. This section will show you how to:

- Use a tool called a proforma to determine if a property is a good investment or not;

- Line up and manage your property manager;
- Have your insurance agent quote you the best policy rate;
- Present your property to a bank to secure a loan; and
- Work with your real estate agent to make an offer based on performance, not emotions.

Let's begin!

CHAPTER 8
Using Numbers-Based Proformas to Identify Strong Investment Properties

In the conventional process of buying real estate, one of the very first steps involves picking up the phone and calling the real estate agent. But my approach is not conventional. Before you call the real estate agent, before you call the property manager, before you call anyone, you need to complete a very important analysis called a property proforma. Essentially, this is a fancy term for the projected performance of a building that you may be interested in purchasing. The bank is going to want to see this information, and having a property proforma will help you avoid spinning your wheels looking any further at buildings that don't meet the specifications of your proforma.

The proforma will help you determine if a property meets your basic business requirements. These should include the following.

- The property will meet the standards for the bank.
- The property will meet the standards for the property manager.
- It's a realistic property for you to invest in.

In a few moments we'll look at a sample property and see exactly how it's done. But before I explain what you *should* do, let's step back for a moment and take a quick look at the traditional way that people approach buying property—and then at how you can use a simple tool called a *proforma* to choose a better method instead.

The Pitfalls of the Conventional Method of Buying Real Estate

You are probably familiar with the traditional method of buying and managing real estate (Figure 7). Let's look at how Mary and Bill might go through this process in the conventional way—and what pitfalls this can entail.

The Buying Process

Figure 7: The Conventional Buying Process

Mary and Bill decide they'd like to invest in residential real estate investing. Mary sees a real estate agent's "for sale" sign on a building she likes and gives that person a call. It turns out that the building is already under contract, but the real estate agent shows Bill and Mary a bunch of similar properties. They aren't really sure how many units they can handle, but they make a guess, picking a number that sounds about right. Eventually, they find a property that seems like a good match, so they go ahead and make an offer. They are outbid by another buyer and they aren't really sure what the property is worth, so they decide to go back to square one.

After viewing several more properties, they find another apartment building that seems suitable and they make another offer, which is accepted. This time, there is an unwelcome surprise during an inspection. The entire property would need to be rewired. Bill and Mary decide they are not ready for this kind of overhaul, so they withdraw their offer and start looking at a bunch of properties again.

Eventually, they find one that seems like it might work. They make another offer. This time it is accepted and the wiring looks good. At this point, they start searching around for bank financing. They're feeling a bit fatigued by the whole process, so they decide to stick with their own savings bank. They are surprised to find that the mortgage application is a long, drawn-out process because the bank wants to see a lot of documentation that they hadn't known they would need to prepare. Eventually, they sort all that out and it's finally time for the closing. The bank chooses a title company, and although Bill and Mary sense that the selection is definitely in the bank's best interest versus their own, they don't have the energy to protest or find their own.

At this point, they also need an insurance agent. Here too, they do the minimum amount of research by selecting the company that already provides them with car insurance.

Bill and Mary finally receive the keys and manage the

property for a few months on their own, but they find that they aren't really prepared to handle unexpected issues. They had forgotten to check the existing leases when they first considered buying the property, so they are caught off guard when several tenants move out, leaving vacant units. They also discover that some of the remaining tenants excel at making excuses to avoid paying the rent on time. In addition, there are necessary repairs that they don't have time to supervise. At this point, they would really like to throw in the towel and sell the property. As a last-ditch attempt to salvage their investment, they call a few property companies and select the one that quotes them the lowest rate. They're not really sure how this will work, but they decide to hope for the best.

The Numbers-Based Approach to Buying Real Estate

As Bill and Mary's example shows, the conventional method of real estate can be long-drawn at best and a full-fledged disaster at worst. But what if you could make a simple decision about a potential investment based on the *actual numbers* involved with the *actual performance of the building*? The good news is that it can.

The property proforma is a tool that allows you to set your criteria and to measure key results and ratios that the bank is going to want to see, that the property manager is going to want to see, and that will drive your real estate agent. It will prevent you from spinning your wheels by helping you focus on viewing only potential properties that you want to see.

Step 1: Basic Information

The first step to completing the proforma is to note the basic information about the property. Figure 8 shows an example.

The first thing to note here is the number of units, because that will affect whether you will pursue *residential financing*, which is used for buildings with four units or fewer, or *commercial financing*, which is required for buildings with five units or more. In this case, it has six units, so it will require commercial financing.

Basic Information

Property Address	123 Great Building Street
# of Units	6
Purchase Price	$360,000.00
Finance Cost	$0.00
Capital Expense Budget	$0.00
Down Payment	$72,000.00
Amount to be Financed	$288,000.00
Total Purchase Price	**$360,000.00**

Figure 8: Property Proforma: Basic Information

The *purchase price* is the next thing to note. A term that I've heard and liked is that you make your profit when you purchase. That is, the purchase price is obviously critical because many of your performance ratios are based on this.

The *finance cost* should also be recorded here. For this example, I've kept it at $0.00. However, when you are considering a building, this will actually include the internal closing costs, such as your attorney's fees and your title company's fees.

In this example I've also kept the capital expense budget

at $0.00. However, with an actual purchase this would involve money that the building would need to address any deferred maintenance or major upgrades that will add longevity and value.

In this example, the down payment is set at 20 percent of the purchase price. As I will discuss in the banking section, it is sometimes possible to get the bank to agree to a lower down payment, or sometimes, based on certain conditions, they may require a higher down payment, but in this case we'll stick with the traditional 20 percent.

That leaves the amount of be financed at $288,000.00. This ties back to what we discussed earlier in the book: the power of leverage. In this case we're buying $360,000.00 worth of property with $72,000.00 of our own money and $288,000.00 of leveraged money.

Step 2: Income of the Building

The next step is to look at the *income of the building* (Figure 9).

Income

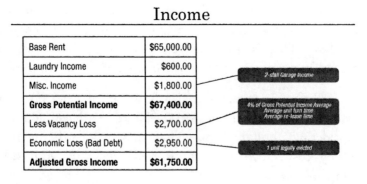

Base Rent	$65,000.00
Laundry Income	$600.00
Misc. Income	$1,800.00
Gross Potential Income	**$67,400.00**
Less Vacancy Loss	$2,700.00
Economic Loss (Bad Debt)	$2,950.00
Adjusted Gross Income	**$61,750.00**

Figure 9: Building Income

This is information that you should request from the real estate agent who is representing the seller *before you even decide to view the property.* Remember the conventional method in which sellers run around viewing a bunch of properties before they even determine if the numbers will work? What you would request is their Schedule E numbers (ask to see an actual copy of the government form), not numbers they have simply placed on a spreadsheet. That is similar to the fine-print term *potential performance.* During this due-diligence step we are looking for actual historical performance.

Let's take a closer look at each thing to consider in the income section of the proforma.

Base Rent

The *base rent* covers how much you would receive if in fact everyone paid on time and all units were occupied.

Laundry Income

This involves additional income such as money from coin-operated laundry facilities.

Miscellaneous Income

In this example, this line accounts for the storage units and garages that can be rented separately from the living units. I highly encourage potential property owners to take advantage of opportunities to make miscellaneous income. Garages and storage units are in high demand.

With that in mind, thinking in terms of redundancies, I never rent out a garage or storage unit to the tenant base within the same building. That might sound strange, but my logic is based on the fact that if tenants aren't paying their rent, it's unlikely they are paying for their parking spot or storage unit either! Some property owners agree with me, while others like to use the storage unit as a marketing feature to help rent the apartment. Ultimately, the choice will be up to you.

Gross Potential Income

This represents what you could make in an ideal situation. That is, always fully occupied, with all residents paying all the time with no break or loss in revenue.

Vacancy Loss

Since the ideal gross potential income may not in fact match what money actually comes in, you would also factor in (and deduct) any potential *vacancy loss*. In this case, we calculated it at 4 percent; some banks calculate it at 5 percent. You will want to confirm this number with someone who has "feet on the street": a local property management firm. Ask for a "localized vacancy rate number." If your area is experiencing a 5 percent vacancy rate citywide, you will want to get a very specific idea of the vacancy rate in your property's immediate vicinity. A good property manager should know almost down to the street level, the average vacancy rate for the neighborhood. (Don't even think about working with any company that cannot provide this information.)

My property management company internally tracks this information, including retention rates, on a quarterly basis. At the time of this writing, my last quarter's vacancy rate number was exactly 4.3% on rentable units. It's important to have these numbers as precise as possible.

Economic Loss

The building we are considering in this example also has a history of *economic loss* that should also be deducted. This results when someone stays in the unit but does not pay the rent. The bank will not calculate for this, but as a hands-on investor, you will want to do the maximum analysis, not the minimum. This situation is often very frustrating, because economic loss, unlike vacancy loss, affects both sides of your profit-and-loss statement. There is no income coming in, yet the tenants are utilizing the facilities of your building, which is creating an expense.

Adjusted Gross Income
These calculations will leave you with your *adjusted gross income*, which is the amount that you are likely to receive from your investment.

Step 3: Operating Expenses

Next, you'll want to take a very close look at the operating expenses of a building (Figure 10). Simply put, the operating expenses include whatever supports the financial viability of the building.

You will want to verify all of these numbers. Ask the real estate agent to get you copies of the following sources.

The rent roll, which is a listing of tenants living in each unit along with their rental rates, security deposits, move-in dates, lease expiration dates, ledger balances, phone numbers, and email addresses.

The actual leases.

The existing owner's Schedule E (see Part II), which will show what the seller is reporting to the government as the operating expenses.

Operating Expenses

Management Fee	$3,705.00	6.00%
Electricty	$600.00	
Heating Fuel	$0.00	
Sewer/Water	$2,675.00	1 unit legally evicted
Insurance	$3,100.00	
Real Estate Taxes	$7,430.00	Estimate, Grounds Maint May - Nov / Snow Removal Dec - Apr
Advertising	$50.00	
Professional Legal Fees	$700.00	
Grounds Maintenance	$500.00	Location Estimate: 5% of GPI
Maintenance & Repairs	$3,370.00	
Avg. Unit Turn Cost	$1,99.00	1-unit turn
Misc. Expenses	$670.00	
Total Operating Expenses	**$24,700.00**	40.00%

Figure 10: Total Operating Expenses

Management Fee

If you choose to use a property management company, then one of your first expenses will be your management fee. In the case of this example, the management fee is set at 6 percent. As I stressed earlier, when you are hiring a management company, try to focus less on how much the fee will be, and more on what you will be getting out of the service. The 6 percent fee could go up to 10 percent in some cases, but it's immaterial to a certain extent. If you have a very cheap deal on a management company but you experience a high rate of vacancies they are not prepared to deal with, then what's the point? I'd rather pay 10 percent and make sure that my building is not vacant, or that there are strategies in place with that particular management company to make sure that my vacancy rates are minimized. But, in the spirit of our example, 6 percent it is!

Utilities

The next expenses are the utilities associated with the

building. I recommend verifying any numbers you are quoted on as to utilities. The best way to verify these numbers is to get them from the real estate agent and to double-check what the seller reported on Schedule E.

One further step you can (and should!) take is to also call the utility companies to verify those numbers. Simply state that you are interested in purchasing this building and that you would like to get an average heating cost or the average bill for the last two or three years.

One more strategy that I recommend involves asking the real estate agent to provide actual invoices to show what the seller paid involving those utility expenses.

Insurance

At this point, it is worth a phone call to some insurance agencies to get an idea of what the potential cost of insurance will be. This will not be set in stone, but if they all come in at around the same figure, it should give you a pretty close idea of what the cost is likely to be.

Real Estate Taxes

Real estate taxes can (and should!) be confirmed by your local tax office. Some towns and cities actually let you review this online; in other cases, you will want to make a phone call or pay a visit to the office.

Advertising

Advertising should be based on how much it would cost you to list a vacant unit.

Legal Fees

The professional legal fees will be the fees incurred for any form of legal representation needed for the property or the entity that you own the property in, such as the fees involved to evict any tenant who is not paying rent (the economic loss mentioned earlier). Your attorney or a potential property management company can provide that number to you. Again, you might want to check with more than one party to ensure that you get an accurate figure.

Grounds Maintenance

These will include grounds maintenance such as snow plowing and shoveling fees if the building is in a cold climate. It will also include lawn mowing, tree trimming, pruning and post-storm cleanups, and so forth.

Maintenance and Repairs

If the building you are considering is a well-maintained, up-to-date property that will meet the insurance requirements (e.g., it has updated plumbing and wiring), then I would estimate this figure at 5 percent of the GPI, the gross potential income (no vacancies, no economic loss). If it's an older building or one with a high volume of turnover, which is typically where you get most of your expenses, then it would rise higher, perhaps up to 15 percent. Historical performance is sometimes a good indicator of future performance.

Average Unit Turn Cost

The *average unit turn cost* is the cost to turn a vacant unit (cleaning, painting, etc.) plus any fees to the management company (if you have one) to re-lease the unit for you.

Miscellaneous Expenses

In terms of *miscellaneous expenses,* I typically run 1 percent of GPI (gross potential income) for any tough-to-categorize and/or unexpected expenses.

This will give you your total operating expenses, which in this case is about 40 percent of the gross potential income. In the New England market that my property company operates in, the average operating expense to gross potential income ratio that I am seeing for older multifamily dwellings average to about 35 percent of gross potential income.

Step 4: Performance Metrics

Figure 11 takes all of these numbers and calculates the estimated cash flow, which is the key figure you'll need to consider to make decisions as you move forward.

These are the numbers that you'll be communicating to your bank, to your property manager, to the seller as you negotiate the price, and perhaps eventually to a buyer if you decide to sell the building.

Let's take a careful look at each of these important numbers.

Performance Metrics

Net Operating Income	$37,050.00	NOI=Adjusted Gross Income - Total Operating Expenses
Debt Services	$20,203.00	5.0% amortized over 25 years
DSCR	1.83	Debt Service Coverage Ratio = NOI/Debt Service. Amount of cash left to service the debt after all operations expenses have been paid
Cap Rate	10.30%	Capitalization Rate = NOI/Purchase Price. Return on Investment
CoC	10.30%	Cash on Cash Return = Cash Flow After Debt Service/Down Payment. Return on Cash vested in property
Cash Flow After Debt Service	**$16,847.00**	Free and Clear Cash Flow or Profit

Figure 11: Performance Metrics

Net Operating Income

By this stage in the book, you should be familiar with the

term *net operating income.* Again, this refers to the adjusted gross income minus the total operating expenses.

Debt Service

The *debt service* actually refers to your annualized mortgage payment. In the figure I've noted that for this example we're looking at a twenty-five year mortgage (which is pretty typical), with a 5 percent interest rate.

Debt Service Coverage Ratio (DSCR)

As you apply for a mortgage, the bank is going to be particularly interested in the ratio called your DSCR, the *debt service coverage ratio.* This is the amount of cash left over, after all of your operating expenses are paid, to pay for your mortgage. This is calculated by taking your NOI (the adjusted gross income minus the total operating expenses) and dividing it by your debt service (mortgage).

In this case, the DSCR is 1.83. That means that for every dollar that you pay to the bank for your mortgage, you have eighty-three cents left over. You have 83 percent more money than you need to pay the bank. Even if things go wrong for a time, you have plenty of money coming in.

Most banks require, at a minimum, a DSCR of 1.25, preferably higher. This means that if you complete a proforma and the DSCR comes out at less than 1.25, you know immediately that either this is the wrong investment for the price point or that you would have to demonstrate to the bank that by adding a certain value (be it increasing rents or decreasing expenses) you can bring that debt service coverage ratio over 1.25.

Cap Rate

The next important ratio is the *cap rate*. The cap rate is defined as the net operating income divided by the purchase price (how much you're making versus how much you're paying).

This is the total return on the investment. Let's say I'm getting a 5 percent total return. The cash flow might look great and the leverage might look great, but if my return is only 5 percent, then I might be better off putting the money in the stock market. It's always important to look at the cap rate before you make any investment decisions.

CoC

The CoC is the cash on cash return (also called the *return on cash*). This looks at your return on the cash you're actually paying. In this case, it was $72,000.00. We want to see what the return on that is. We calculate it by your cash flow after your debt service (mortgage) divided by your down payment. In this case, 23.40 percent looks like a great return on the investment.

Cash Flow After Debt Service

Again, this is your free and clear profit. The bank will want to make sure you have plenty of extra money on hand—and so will you!

So there you have it, the property proforma. This amazing tool takes away the guesswork from real estate property investment and presents you (and your core support team) with the cold, hard facts—the numbers that will determine if the property purchase would be a good investment or not. To me, the property in the example looks like a phenomenal investment.

CHAPTER 9
Lining Up a Property Manager

Now that you've determined that a property will be a good investment, you will want to line up a property manager. *I strongly suggest that you take this step even if you initially think you may want to manage the property yourself.*

There are several reasons for this. First, remember the *Job* portion of the title. Since you will want to keep your job, you may not always have the time it will take to manage your property effectively.

Second, even if you think you will be able to hold your job and manage this property, you will want to know your options if that doesn't work out or if you decide to take on more properties in the future. Remember the scalability plan? Hiring a property manager can be a key component to this.

Third, as you consider whether or not you'll want to manage your own building, you will also want to be able to make the best-informed decision. That will involve gathering some details and numbers from a property manager.

At the least, going through the questions highlighted in this section will remind you of the various tasks involved in property management. For instance, once you review the

questions and see the desired numbers, you may decide that
the price of hiring someone with experience in the field to
handle retentions and vacancies efficiently far outweighs
the cost and the risk of dealing with these potentially costly
issues yourself.

Finally, having a professional property manager onboard
will also reassure the bank that your investment will be
successful. You will want to include this information in your
cover letter when you apply for a mortgage (see Chapter 11).

I suggest that one of the best ways to approach a property
manager is by writing a letter such as the one shown in Figure 12.

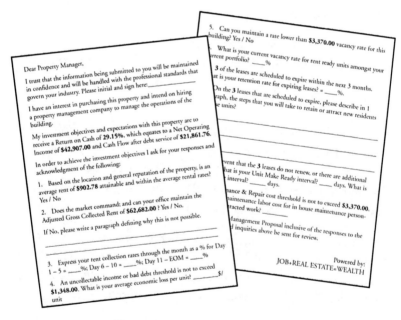

Figure 12: Letter to a property manager

As I've mentioned throughout the book, the hiring process

should be a lot more detailed than simply asking, "What's your fee?" When you get a response to your letter, examine each reply carefully. Remember, you are not asking the property manager to define these terms for you. You have to define the conditions you expect your team to uphold. It's your business, and it's your building.

Let's take a closer look at what each portion of the letter entails.

Opening Lines

The opening lines let the property manager know that he or she will be working with a knowledgeable investor. You are someone who will serve as the team's leader. Right off the bat you are educating your potential property manager on what you are looking for and what you will expect.

Rent Collection Numbers

It will be essential for you to determine how effective the property manager has been at collecting the rent for other clients. The letter requests percentages for days 1–5, 6–10, and 11–EOM (end of month). At my management firm, we track our collection numbers by quarter, and we actually have it broken up by days within the month, by segments within the month. I aim to have 98 percent of the rent in hand by the end of the month. If a property manager does not or cannot give you those numbers, that is a matter of concern. Specifically, if the property manager doesn't know what those numbers are or can't respond to that question, the firm might not be able to collect that kind of income for you.

Adjusted Gross Collected Rent

Similarly, for this example you will want to make sure that the market can support, and their office can maintain, an adjusted gross income of $61,750.00. This is a simple "yes" or "no" question, and a good sanity check and litmus test of you, the buyer. Does the building support a projected income of $61,750.00 in rent, or is this a location where no management company could collect that kind of income?

Vacancy Rate

The next requirement to express is your vacancy rate for this building. If your aim is 4 percent (remember, you are driving your team) and the property manager has a track record with other buildings of 10 percent, this relationship won't be a good match.

Policy for Expiring Leases

The retention rate is another significant issue. In my office, I focus on my retention rate strategies. It costs a lot to turn a unit, it costs a lot to market that unit, and it costs a lot to show the unit and get a good tenant in there. So, be sure that you are happy with the answers about strategies and incentives for retention. In my company, we are able to retain 97 percent of our tenants, with 3 percent moving out of the area, buying a home, or going to a competitor.

Unit Make-Ready Interval

Once a unit becomes vacant, how long does it take to get the unit prepped up for re-lease? Turnaround time is crucial. My company allows for an approximate one-week turnaround between tenants, which involves painting and unit maintenance. This is a good window of time, and you will certainly not want it to be any longer than that. Remember, when you add in the advertising, unit showings, and successful lease negotiations, it means that you are losing approximately one month of rent every time a tenant leaves.

Uncollectible Income Maximum

This is really a statement. You want to make sure they have an aggressive collection standpoint if the tenant does not pay swiftly. You want them to have a legal plan in process to evict tenants as needed. Again, you are driving the property manager's behavior. It's your business; it's your building.

Maintenance and Repair Threshold

Also make sure your property manager can maintain a certain maintenance threshold. Again, for the purposes of this building, let's put the threshold at $3,370.00. It is important to be specific with these numbers so the expenses don't run over. It's a good idea to incentivize keeping the costs under this threshold, such as offering the company a bonus to be distributed each year that the costs are down. This is very worthwhile in the long run.

Management and Leasing Fees

You will want to set this fee based on your relationship with the property manager and your expectations.

Conflict Resolution Process

You will also want to carefully examine the property manager's conflict resolution process for the residents of the building. Lack of tenant relations resolution is one of the most common reasons given for tenants to move, and you will want to make sure the management has a strategy and accountability for these issues. In my business, we have a dedicated Resident Relations Department to deal with conflict resolution and communication.

Owner Communication and Notification Process

If you decide to hire the property management company, as part of the contract you will want to cosign a statement defining the owner communications and notification process. This is really important. In addition to giving the management company your expectations on cash, retention, and expense budgets, here you want to know how the company plans to communicate with you about these issues moving forward. You want to remain deeply involved in the workings of the building management. Remember, real estate is a working asset. You need to be involved, and you need to manage your property manager. The property manager is the facilitator, but ultimately, as owner of the building, you have to be the decision maker.

This letter is simple but effective. It takes you from a position of being a recipient of services to driving behavior of services. You are driving potential property managers to run your building with analytics and specifics—a surefire path to success.

CHAPTER 10
Working with Insurance Agents to Get the Best Rates Possible

Insurance is another area in which it pays for you to understand the industry. The key question is this: What criteria do insurance agencies look for to quote insurance? Yes, insurance companies are there to protect your interests, but the bottom line is that the first concern is protecting themselves. They don't want you to have a claim because they don't want to have to pay out on a claim.

To minimize their risk, the first thing they do once you bind coverage is send a risk assessor to look at the property. That person goes through the building and then lets the insurance company know what potential risks and hazards exist with the property. Those risks and hazards are what they'll use to determine the insurance rate.

As an example, let's think about a building in the Northeast that has a flat roof. Since the weight of excessive snow can cause undue stress on such a roof, the risk of collapse is evaluated by the insurance company. They won't necessarily deny coverage (although some will), but they will likely charge you a premium.

The key is to think like an insurance assessor before you make an offer on a property. Call up some local agencies and ask what criteria they use to make an assessment. Most likely, you will come up with a list similar to the one included in the letter shown in Figure 13.

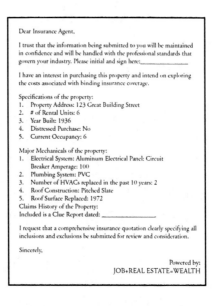

Dear Insurance Agent,

I trust that the information being submitted to you will be maintained in confidence and will be handled with the professional standards that govern your industry. Please initial and sign here:_____

I have an interest in purchasing this property and intend on exploring the costs associated with binding insurance coverage.

Specifications of the property:
1. Property Address: 123 Great Building Street
2. # of Rental Units: 6
3. Year Built: 1936
4. Distressed Purchase: No
5. Current Occupancy: 6

Major Mechanicals of the property:
1. Electrical System: Aluminum Electrical Panel: Circuit Breaker Amperage: 100
2. Plumbing System: PVC
3. Number of HVACs replaced in the past 10 years: 2
4. Roof Construction: Pitched Slate
5. Roof Surface Replaced: 1972
Claims History of the Property:
Included is a Clue Report dated: _____

I request that a comprehensive insurance quotation clearly specifying all inclusions and exclusions be submitted for review and consideration.

Sincerely,

Powered by:
JOB+REAL ESTATE=WEALTH

Figure 13: Insurance Company Letter

Before you set up an insurance binder with any company, you will want to take the list and go through the property yourself. Let's say the numbers on the proforma are great, but you realize that the building has hazardous wiring. At that point, because you haven't purchased the property, there are steps that you can still take. For instance, you may decide to pull out of the deal and find another property. Or, you may want to get estimates to rewire the building and then negotiate that cost out of the purchase price when you make the offer.

Either way, you will once again be making a decision that's as fact-based as possible.

Most of the items on the list are self-explanatory, but again, you may want to do some more research on specific items such as plumbing and wiring. Let's look at a few more of the items here.

Vacancies

One factor that insurance companies look for is current vacancies. Vacancies pose a risk because often the buildings are a target for vandalism.

Physical Attributes

This includes the electrical, plumbing, and heating systems. The answers to these questions often reflect the overall condition of the building.

Certificate of Compliance

This states to the insurance company that a city official has inspected the building and deemed it safe from an occupancy standpoint. This is only applicable if the city, town or municipality enforces a housing code inspection. It would be wise to inquire about the frequency of these inspections and if applicable, the results of the last inspection.

Proposed Use

Insurance companies also want to know if you plan to utilize the building in its current use or if you plan to rehab the building. This is a concern to them because if you turn the building into a construction zone, even temporarily, they may find themselves facing claims from workers who have an accident onsite and don't have adequate coverage of their own.

So there you have it. As you complete the letter, be sure to disclose any concerns that you have. Again, you want to drive what occurs—in this case the rate that they offer you based on the fact-based situation you present to them—not be a passive recipient.

CHAPTER 11
Presenting the Property to the Bank to Secure a Loan

Now that you've picked out a potential property, run the numbers, and lined up your property management and insurance team, you'll want to pick up the phone and call the real estate agent and make an offer. Right?

The answer is still *not yet*. The next step is to get the financing approved. It's time to take your proforma and write a letter to the bank (Figure 14).

The first three paragraphs list the location and explain that you would like to build a relationship with the bank. Remember, the bank is going to be a member of your team. Here too, you will want to *lead* that relationship as a driving force, not act as a passive recipient.

The fourth paragraph provides very clearly, up front, the main numbers that the bank will be interested in. These include the following.

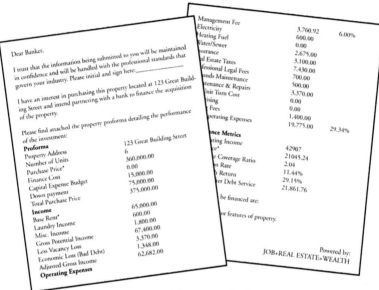

Figure 14: Letter to a Banker

- The net operating income, which shows that the property is profitable;

- The mortgage amount requested;

- The amount of your down payment, which assures them that you have a personal interest in making the property succeed;

- The DSCR (Debt Service Coverage Ratio), which shows that the bank will be in a very secure position (again the magic number they'll look for is 1.25, so do not move forward if the number is lower than that, unless of course you have a plan that you can demonstrate to the bank will raise the DSCR to north of 1.25);

- The return on cash (CoC), which shows you'll have extra cash in hand after paying the mortgage;

- The cap rate, which shows that it's a strong investment for you and a secure risk for them.

In today's economy, risk assessment for a bank is huge. They want to be sure you are in a secure position, which your $72,000.00 down payment affords you. The debt service coverage ratio shows the bank that should they need to foreclose on the building in the future, the building can still stand on its own two feet, meaning that they will be able to resell the property relatively easily. But more important, if the bank sees that you will be getting a 23 percent return on your cash, the bank knows that you will be doing well and will be unlikely to walk away.

The next line states the requested interest rate and the length of the mortgage. Remember, the returns of investment that we have outlined here are based on getting a mortgage with an interest rate of 5 percent amortized over twenty-five years. When contacting the bank, it is important to drive their behavior. Instead of asking the banker for their terms, show them what you are requesting, and prove that you've already done your homework, and are serious.

Be sure to communicate which insurance and property management professionals you plan to sign on to your team. This shows the bank that you've done your homework, you understand their industry, and you know what you're talking about.

Finally, you should request that, if market conditions are favorable, you want to receive better rates for this loan. There's no harm in asking, and it's another step in which you can drive the behavior of the bank versus the other way around.

When you send the letter, be sure to include a copy of the entire proforma. This will show the bank the full set of figures, and again it will assure them that should they ever need to foreclose, the building performs well in terms of income generation and should be easy for them to sell again.

CHAPTER 12
Working with your Real Estate Agent to Make an Offer

Finally, it is time for you to work with your real estate agent to make an offer. Up to this point, of course, you have probably worked with the real estate agent to a certain degree, such as when you met to inspect the property and when you required documents from the seller's real estate agent, such as copies of the existing leases. But unlike buyers who take the conventional approach, you have not let the real estate agent lead you from building to building based on what he or she thinks you need—or based on what he or she most needs to sell. From the very start you have taken the lead, and you will continue to do so now.

The first step you will want to take is to write a letter such as the one shown in Figure 15. The letter shows that you are a serious buyer who is making an offer based on facts, not emotions. It's purely a business decision.

Dear Real Estate Sales Agent,

I trust that the information being submitted to you will be maintained in confidence and will be handled with the professional standards that govern your industry. Please initial and sign here:______________

I have an interest in purchasing residential properties that meet similar performance and physical specifications:

Apartment Buildings: **All Residential**
Number of units: **6**
With a down payment not to exceed **$75,000.00**
Debt Service Coverage Ratio: **2.04**
Capitalization Rate: **11.44%**
Cash on Cash Return: **29.15%**

I require that prior to any letter of intent to purchase be constructed, the following be supplied for my review:

Property rent-roll detailing lease start and end dates, lease amounts and any special inclusions (such as utilities). In particular the 4 leases expiring.
12-month Operating Statement or Profit & Loss statement
Schedule E's for 2 previous tax periods
A Clue Report from the current Insurance carrier for the last 2yrs

Sincerely

Powered by:
JOB+REAL ESTATE=WEALTH

Figure 15: Letter to Real Estate Agent

As you can see, the letter begins with the same type of confidentiality statement that should be included in the letters to the property manager and the insurance agent. Then you identify the property location and note that you are including the building's proforma. Again, this indicates to your real estate agent (and the seller) that you have done your homework; they are working with an informed, professional buyer. It also ensures that sellers won't be able to take offense when you make an offer, because you have ample statistics and information to substantiate your claims. Your offer is based on performance, not on emotion.

The next line continues to show that you are firmly in the driving seat. You explain what return on cash and return on cash that you are looking for, and then you list the purchase price that will allow you to achieve those numbers. Again, this places the offer in the realm of concrete financial results, not emotions.

The next lines state your expectations for the seller in terms of actions you want to see taken before the sale is finalized. Of course, this will vary from situation to situation, but in general you will want to request that the seller perform the following duties or credit you appropriately on your purchase agreement.

- Renegotiate any departing tenants' leases or non-performing tenants' leases to ensure that they're extended or terminated respectively;

- Perform any necessary enhancements and renovations to any soon-to-be vacated units (if the leases cannot be extended);

- Correct any liabilities uncovered during the inspection to correct any insurance violations;

- Make any outstanding updates or improvements that need to be made to the property.

As this chapter has shown, working with a real estate agent is all about educating yourself, clearly communicating your needs and objectives, and making sure that your decisions are made on facts, not emotions. Before you know it, you will have the keys to start your path as a residential real estate investor right in your hands.

CONCLUSION

Before I say goodbye, let's quickly summarize what you've learned in this program. In the first part, you learned that in order to maintain your job and get into real estate, you need to develop the right mindset. We discussed the benefits of residential real estate investments, and we went through five different personality types. You learned that while all of these types have good qualities, the goal is to become a blended business personality type—someone who can analyze data, has plenty of confidence, can build a good team, and listens to gut feelings.

We also went through the process wheel. You can use the process wheel to make smart choices any time you are faced with a problem or need to make a decision. Here you learned to identify your investment strategy, come up with an execution approach, measure your success so you can learn from your mistakes, and obtain the necessary support to allow you to achieve your goals. All plans to need to be scalable to ensure that your investment returns are steady and can be replicated in the future if you wish to do so.

In Part II of the program, we talked about the financial benefits of real estate. We identified cash flow, leverage, and tax benefits—all compelling reasons to invest in real estate.

Again, we are becoming a nation of renters, and it can always be a great time to get into the real estate market.

Finally, we rolled up our sleeves and got into the finer points of how to analyze the property using a tool called a proforma and how to drive the behavior of your core success team. We identified the best ways to work with a property manager, an insurance agent, a banker, and a real estate agent to ensure that you are the one leading the team.

In the future, I would love to hear your success stories. Please feel free to contact me at: **francis.fernando@totalsolutionspm.com**. Regular updates to this material will also appear on my website to help you keep current and focused. Take some time to visit the website at **www.francisfernando.com.**

Now go out there with confidence, identify a property, execute a purchase plan, measure how that property gets you closer towards your goal and compile your support team. **Good luck!**

GLOSSARY

Adjusted gross income—the actual revenue you are able to collect from a property

Bank-owned properties—real estate assets that are owned by the bank after a foreclosure sale

Business Process Wheel—a tool to help users form an investment plan by following four steps: identify, execute, measure, and support.

Capital appreciation—the rise in the asset's value based on a rise in market price

Capital expense budget—the money a building would potentially need in order to take care of any deferred maintenance. This is needed to keep the asset at optimal market value

Cash flow—your profit, which is based on the income from rent checks that remains after the internal expenditures from running the building, your taxes, insurance and your mortgage payment

Commercial financing—a loan or mortgage that is typically written for businesses, commercial properties or large residential properties (typically 4-units and greater)

Core success team—the critical members of your team that will drive the results you strive. For the context of this book your core success team is your real estate agent, banker, insurance agent, and property manager

Depreciation—the IRS defines this as "an annual allowance for the wear and tear, deterioration, or obsolescence of the property"

Economic loss—is the loss of revenue or rents due to market conditions. This could be in the form of concessions offered in order to keep the renters in the building to write-offs due to uncollectable rent.

Gross potential income—the sum of all the potential sources of income for the property. Typically, they are the base rent, laundry income, and any other miscellaneous income such as storage facilities

Leasing fee—a brokerage fee typically assessed by a property manager or real estate broker to facilitate and secure a new lease for a vacant unit

Leverage position—the use of borrowed capital, such as a mortgage, to increase the potential return of an investment

Maintenance threshold—a value established by the owner of the property and communicated to the property manager as a maximum or minimum threshold to maintain for routine maintenance expenses over a fixed period

Master lease—a primary lease that controls any subsequent leases written on the leased premises

Net operating income—the difference between what rent you collect and the operational expenses incurred to run the property

Property proforma—the projected performance of the building. This can be based on historical performance of the building and/or current and anticipated market conditions

Rent roll—a listing of tenants living in each unit, along with their rental rates, security deposits, move-in dates, lease expiration dates, ledger balances, phone numbers, and email addresses

Residential financing—a loan used to secure real property to be used as a personal residence or for investment purposes (typically 1 to 4 units)

Scalability plan—a way to adapt to increased growth and demands without making steps too complicated, costly, or hard to manage; the systematic, process-oriented ability to replicate and duplicate the desired economic outcome of an initiative over and over again.

Stable property—for the context of this book, stable properties are able to output a consistent, steady stream of cash-flow due to the make-up of tenants being stable/long-term along with very little or no deferred maintenance on the property

Tax write-off—a reduction in your taxable position based on money taken off the income you make

Unstable property—for the context of this book, unstable properties have erratic cash-flow outputs due to the make-up of tenants being either short-term and/or unpredictable. Furthermore, unstable properties usually have significant deferred maintenance issues

ABOUT THE AUTHOR

Francis Fernando is the President and Founder of Total Solutions Property Management, a thriving Real Estate Asset Management Company, as well as a real estate investor, author, speaker, entrepreneur and coach.

Fernando started Total Solutions Property Management in 2006, and under his expert leadership, the company has grown from a small start-up firm to a highly successful, profitable, well-respected real estate investment business. Total Solutions Property Management now manages more than 500 residential units and represents prestigious, high-profile clients, including US Bank, Wells Fargo, California National Bank and other local, national and international investors and investments firms.

In addition to running his lucrative company, Fernando has built a successful JOB + REAL ESTATE = WEALTH approach, which includes a methodology, training program and book by the same name. The concept is simple - keep your "day job," learn to make smart real estate investments "on the side" and acquire more wealth. Fernando elevated his real estate business using this approach, and is now teaching "regular" people how to become successful "part-time" real estate investors, as well. He educates and empowers people, offering expert tips, advice and best practices to maximize their successes.

Prior to founding Total Solutions, Fernando was a senior engineer at Verizon Communications, a Fortune 500 company. Fernando earned a Bachelor of Science in Electrical & Computer Engineering and a Master of Engineering from the State University of New York at Buffalo. He applies the systematic processes from his engineering background to maximize his successes in the real estate industry.

A native of Buffalo, NY, Fernando has also lived in Central Africa, East Asia and Canada. Fernando, who has dual US-Canadian citizenship, currently lives in Manchester, New Hampshire with his wife and two sons.

CPSIA information can be obtained at www.ICGtesting.com
Printed in the USA
LVOW10s0823010414

379680LV00032BB/1435/P